Let's Start! ICT

Using Instructions

Anne Rooney

QED Publishing

Written by Anne Rooney
Consultant Philip Stubbs
Designed by Jacqueline Palmer
Editor Louisa Somerville
Illustrator John Haslam
Photographer Ray Moller
Models provided by Scallywags

Publisher Steve Evans
Creative Director Louise Morley
Editorial Manager Jean Coppendale

Words in bold **like this** are explained in the Glossary on page 30.

Contents

About Using Instructions

All around you there are objects that are **controlled** by **instructions**. The **remote control** for your TV follows instructions.

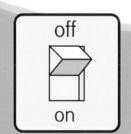

At the flick of a switch

Some things are controlled by a simple switch or button. You turn on a light using a switch. A remote control plane moves at the flick of a switch, too.

Following instructions

Sometimes, pressing a button starts a set of instructions.

When you want to cross the road, you press the button for the lights at the crossing.

The traffic lights follow instructions to switch to red and the cars stop.

The crossing light switches to green and you can cross the road.

In this book, you'll find out how instructions can be used to make things happen.

Taking control

Think of some things you control – such as electronic toys, TVs, DVD players and even a toaster.

Ways of controlling things

We control things in lots of ways. Some things have switches or buttons, and some have dials to turn. Other things have a remote control, so that you can control them without touching them.

What's happening?

Sometimes you have to press a button or a switch for each action.

You might press one button to make a remote control car go forwards and another button to make it turn left or right.

At other times, one action makes a machine do a series of things – setting the video to record, for example.

The video has instructions stored inside it. When you set it to start, it works through them in order.

Do as you're told!

If your teacher says 'put your books away' and you do it, you're following an instruction. But sometimes you might not do as you're told.

Good machine!

Machines are different – they always do as they're told.

When you turn the washing machine on, all you have to do is choose a setting.

You don't need to tell the washing machine to do each thing – it follows a **sequence** of instructions stored inside it.

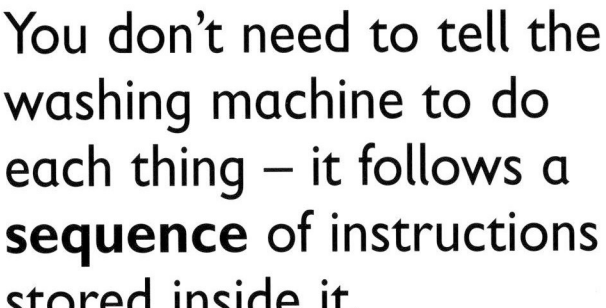

The washing machine fills with water, warms it up, adds the washing powder, churns the clothes around and drains the water away.

It rinses the clothes and spins them to get the water out.

Washing machines usually have more than one set of instructions so they can do different kinds of washing. These instructions are called **programs**.

All in order

Usually, instructions have to be followed in the right order or they won't work.

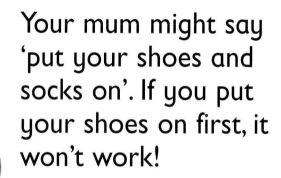

Your mum might say 'put your shoes and socks on'. If you put your shoes on first, it won't work!

If she says 'put your hat and coat on', it doesn't matter which you put on first. The instructions can be followed in any order.

Step by step

Suppose you want to record someone singing a song, using a tape recorder.

You must do it in this order:

- **Put the tape in.**
- **Press the Record button.**
- **Get the person to sing.**
- **Press the Stop button when they finish.**
- **Press Rewind.**
- **Press Play to listen to the song.**

It won't work if you press the buttons in any other order, or if you miss any out.

Start counting

Instructions often include numbers. When you warm a snack in the microwave, you tell the microwave how long to heat it for. If you choose the wrong number, it may burn or be too cold!

Turtles – and friends

It's time to practise working with instructions. At school, you might use a floor turtle – a small machine that follows instructions to move around on the floor.

If you don't have a floor turtle, you can use a friend!

Go!
Tell your friend to go forwards. What happens? They could keep going until they walk into something. The same will happen with the floor turtle.

It's better to say how far, using a number. If you tell your friend (or turtle) to go forwards three spaces, you know just how far they will go.

If you're using a friend, it's easiest if you work on a floor that has tiles or paving stones all the same size.

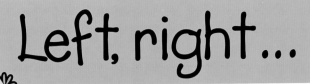

Left, right...

One instruction is a good start – but a whole set of instructions will make something more interesting happen.

Which direction?

To make your friend or turtle go somewhere that isn't in a straight line, you'll need to tell them when to turn corners.

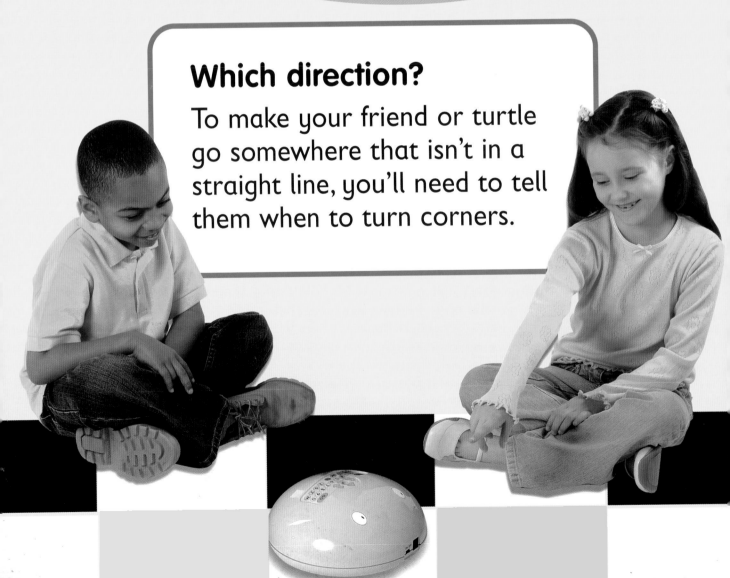

To the finish

Imagine you want your friend to go to a chair. You could say 'go forwards three, turn left, go forwards four'. If you write down your instructions, you can use them again.

Break it up

Write each instruction on a new line to make them clear.

Go forwards 3
Turn left
Go forwards 4

Here are the steps your friend takes to follow the instructions:

Start here

Follow the leader

A second friend could follow the same instructions to get to the same place.

Turning

You can turn all the way around, or you can turn part way. Knowing how far to turn is important when you give or follow instructions.

Full turn

A full turn means you turn all the way round. At the end, you'll face the same way as when you started!

Half turn

If you turn halfway round, you'll face the opposite way when you stop.

It doesn't matter whether you turn left or right – you face the same way in the end.

Quarter turn

After a quarter turn, you'll face right or left. To turn left, hold out your left arm by raising it to the side of your body.

Now turn to face the way your arm was pointing. You can put your arm down!

You've turned a quarter of the way round.

If you did two quarter turns, you'd have done a half turn.

If you did it four times, you would have done a full turn. You would be facing the same way as when you started.

Start from here

Instructions only work properly if you start from the right place.

Go forwards 2
Turn left
Go forwards 1

Get it right!

The instructions to get to the chair (see page 15) won't work if your friend starts on the wrong square. Following the same instructions, they'll get to somewhere else.

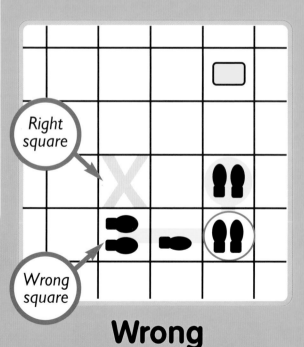

Right square

Wrong square

Wrong

You'd need different instructions if your friend started here.

The new instructions would be:

> Go forwards 2
> Turn left
> Go forwards 2

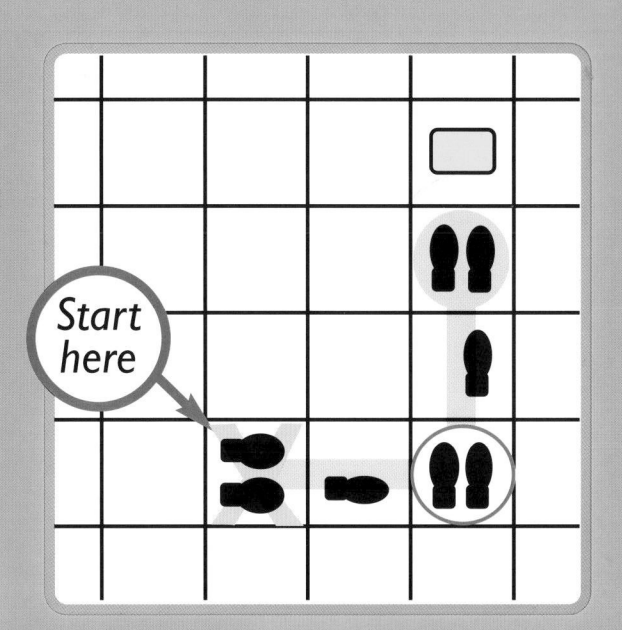

Right

Mystery tour

Send your friend or turtle on a mystery tour! Pick a direction, right or left, and throw a dice to see how many steps they take.

Do it ten times. Write down the route they take like this, with arrows to show left and right:

Make it clear

Instructions must be really clear so that people – or turtles – can follow them properly.

The right words...

When you talk to a friend, he or she understands all the words you say. You can say the same thing in different ways.

Machines aren't as clever. They don't know as many words. Your turtle knows only a few words, so you have to use the right ones.

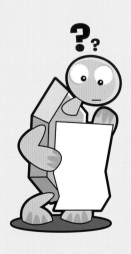

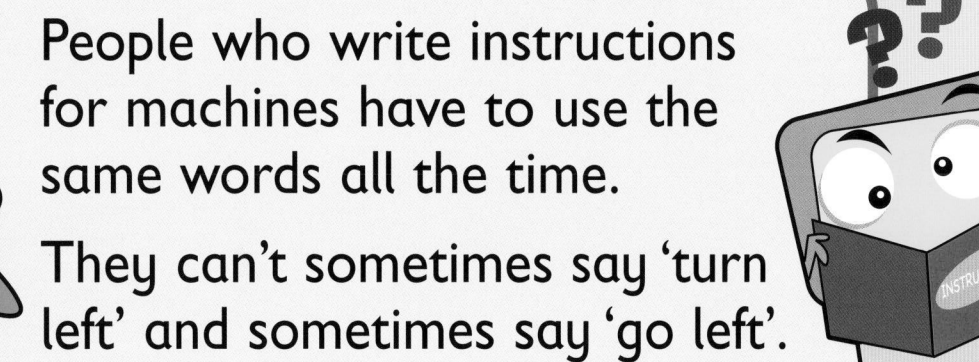

People who write instructions for machines have to use the same words all the time.

They can't sometimes say 'turn left' and sometimes say 'go left'.

Numbers

You must be clear when you use numbers, too. If you say 'go forward 1' to a friend, they won't know if you mean one step or one kilometre!

Your floor turtle always goes the same distance for the same number. It doesn't know that there are different ways to measure distance.

Turning turtle

Your turtle only understands a few words. It has buttons labelled with the words it knows.

'Right 1', or 'Rt 1', turns the turtle to the right a quarter turn like this:

'Left 1', or 'Lt 1', turns the turtle to the left a quarter turn like this:

'Forward 1', or 'Fd 1', tells the turtle to go forward one step.

Here are some instructions for two routes. Get your friend – or turtle – to follow them.

Forward 4
Right 1
Forward 10
Right 1
Forward 4

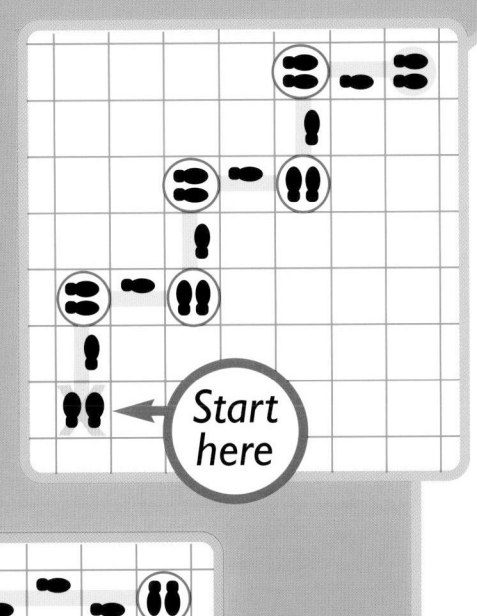

Start here

Forward 2
Right 1
Forward 2
Left 1
Forward 2
Right 1
Forward 2
Left 1
Forward 2
Right 1
Forward 2

Start here

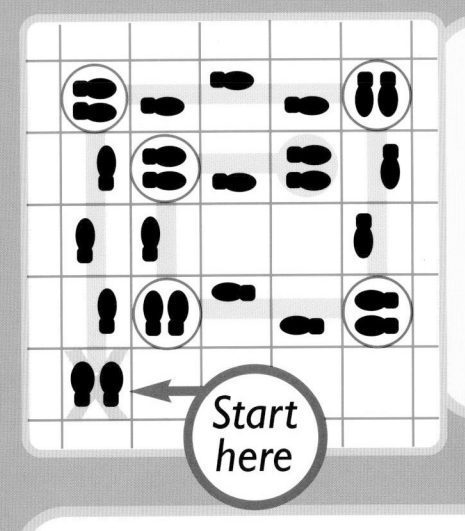

Start here

Can you work out the instructions for this route?

The answer is at the bottom of the page.

Answer: Forward 4, Right 1, Forward 4, Right 1, Forward 3, Right 1, Forward 3, Right 1, Forward 2, Right 1, Forward 1, Right 1, Forward 2

Again and again

Sometimes you need to use the same instruction twice or more. One way is to give the instruction all over again.

Round and round

You could use these instructions to make your friend or turtle go round in a square.

Forward 3
Right 1
Forward 3
Right 1
Forward 3
Right 1
Forward 3
Right 1

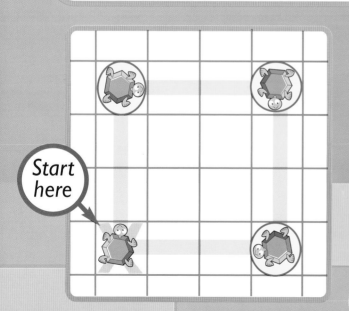

Start here

Your turtle will have a **repeat** button on it.

You can use this to tell it to repeat a set of actions.

Forward 3
Right 1

If the turtle repeats these steps three times, it will draw a square.

Work it out

If you know the starting place you can work out what a set of instructions will do.

Where will the turtle end up if it follows these instructions twice?

Forward 2
Right 1
Forward 2
Left 1

Practise!

Find out how to make your turtle repeat steps. Which buttons do you have to press?

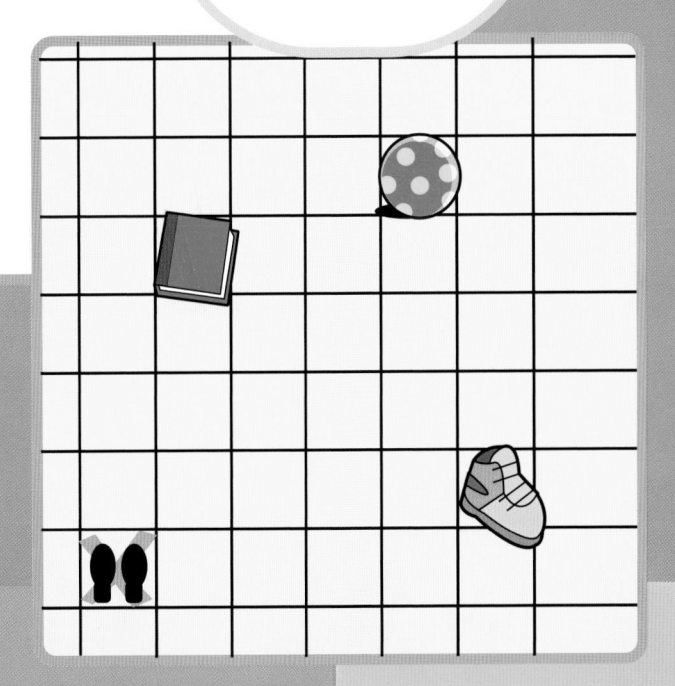

Answer: The turtle ends up in the square below the ball.

Over to you

Now it's time to do some work of your own. You'll need a friend. If you've got a turtle, you can use that, too.

Being a robot

Robots can only follow instructions. Use the turtle (or your friend) as a robot.

If your friend is the robot, tell them to follow your instructions exactly, even if the instructions are wrong!

Hidden treasure

1. Put three boxes upside down on the floor and hide something under one of them.

2. Write a set of instructions to get your friend or turtle to the treasure box.

3. Show your friend the starting place and the instructions to reach the hidden treasure.

4. Then test the instructions. Either get your friend to follow them, or program the turtle to follow them.

Was the treasure found? If not, how do you need to change the instructions?

Start here

Draw-o-matic

The draw-o-matic draws a picture by following your instructions!

You'll need:
a friend
2 pencils
6 sheets of squared paper

Plan a picture

Each of you draw a picture on squared paper. Make sure you don't see each other's drawings.

- You can draw only along the edges of the squares, not across them.

- Each line must be a whole number of squares long.

- You have to keep the pencil on the paper. You can go over the same line twice.

Your turn, my turn

The instructions for the drawing must start from the bottom left corner, going up.

Here's one for you and your friend to practise:

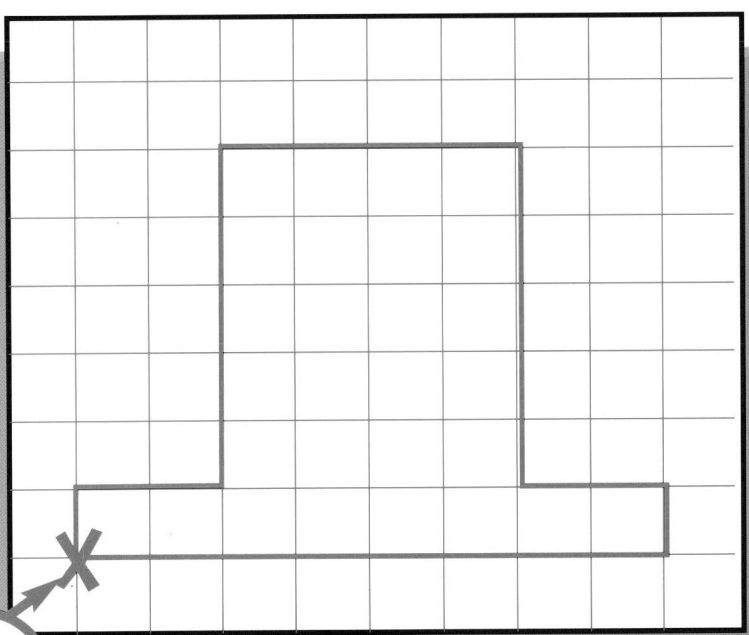

Start
here

Forward 1
Right 1
Forward 2
Left 1
Forward 5
Right 1
Forward 4
Right 1
Forward 5
Left 1
Forward 2
Right 1
Forward 1
Right 1
Forward 8

Now write instructions for your own drawings.

Swap instructions and be a draw-o-matic! When you've done it, look at what you've both drawn.

Did you both draw the right shapes?

29

Glossary

control Make something do what you want it to do.

instructions Words or actions that tell someone or something what to do.

program Set of instructions for a machine, such as a computer, to follow.

remote control Box with buttons that let you control something, like a TV or video player. The instructions are sent through the air from the box to the object that it controls.

repeat Do a series of actions more than once.

robot Machine that is controlled by instructions or a computer.

sequence Set or series of steps that must be done in order.

Index

Grown-up zone

Using Instructions
and the National Curriculum

The work in this book will help children to cover the following parts of the National Curriculum ICT scheme of work: unit 1f and unit 2d.

It can be tied in with work on geography, literacy, maths, science, design technology and any other area of the curriculum in which the children can think about following and designing sets of instructions.

If a floor turtle is not available, a screen turtle can be used. A downloadable version of the programming language LOGO can be obtained from: www.softronix.com/logo.html

Encourage children to work together and discuss how to sequence instructions so that they are precise and not ambiguous. Make sure they are aware that the starting position will affect the outcome of directions involving movement.

Children should be encouraged to review, evaluate and improve their own work at all stages. When working with instructions, you can introduce the idea of testing and revising the sequence to make corrections.

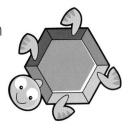